FIRST-PERSON STORIES OF THE
HOLOCAUST

BY NICOLE HORNING

ROSEN PUBLISHING PRIMARY SOURCE LIBRARY

ROSEN PUBLISHING

Published in 2027 by The Rosen Publishing Group, Inc.
2544 Clinton Street, Buffalo, NY 14224

Designer: Deanna Lepovich
Editor: Nicole Horning

Library of Congress Cataloging-in-Publication Data

Names: Horning, Nicole author
Title: First-person stories of the Holocaust / Nicole Horning.
Description: Buffalo, NY : Rosen Publishing, [2027] | Series: The rosen publishing primary source library | Includes index.
Identifiers: LCCN 2026009361 | ISBN 9781725342842 library binding | ISBN 9781725342835 paperback | ISBN 9781725342859 ebook
Subjects: LCSH: Holocaust, Jewish (1939-1945) | World War, 1939-1945–Underground movements | Nazi concentration camps
Classification: LCC D804.34 .H68 2027 | DDC 940.53/18–dc23/eng/20260401
LC record available at https://lccn.loc.gov/2026009361

Some of the images in this book illustrate individuals who are models. The depictions do not imply actual situations or events.

Manufactured in the United States of America

CPSIA Compliance Information: Batch #CSRYA27. For further information, contact Rosen Publishing at 1-800-237-9932.

CONTENTS

FOREWORD

History is so much more than just a boring collection of names and dates. It is a collection of stories—sometimes tragic stories, sometimes heroic stories, sometimes romantic stories, sometimes scary stories. And they're all stories of real people who lived real lives.

Those stories can get lost in the shuffle of memorizing battles, studying maps, and listing important court cases or rulers. That's why primary sources are so valuable. They remind us that historical events happened to and because of real people. Reading diaries, looking at photographs, and seeing newspaper articles are just some ways to make history feel personal through primary sources.

Another way is through watching or listening to interviews with people who lived through major historical events. That's what you're invited to do in this book—and all the books that are part of the *Rosen Publishing Primary Source Library*. Each chapter includes quotes from an interview with a real person who experienced a major historical event in a deeply personal way. You can also scan the QR code included at the beginning of each chapter to watch a video interview with the person featured in that chapter.

Created in partnership with Generations Broadcasting, the *Rosen Publishing Primary Source Library* was created to remind readers that there is power in sharing our stories. First-person stories make history come alive. And when history comes alive, we're better able to learn from it—and avoid the mistakes of the past.

The events you're living through today will be part of the next generation's history lessons. As you read and watch the stories collected here, think about what you want your story to be.

Note: More interviews about the topics featured in this series, as well as many other historical events, can be accessed via a subscription to Rosen Publishing's GBC Stories Database: rosendigital.com/GBCStories/.

HOW TO WATCH THE INTERVIEWS FEATURED IN THIS BOOK

- Use your phone's camera, and hold it over the QR code.
- Click the link that appears.
- Watch the video that pops up. If you would like to read a transcript of the interview while you watch, you can click on that option in the video player.

INTRODUCTION

The Holocaust is perhaps the most horrifying event in world history, and it still has an impact today on survivors, their children and grandchildren, and the entire Jewish population. For 12 years, from 1933 through 1945, the Jewish people were systematically **persecuted**, their way of life significantly altered before they were put onto trains, taken to camps such as concentration camps and death camps, and murdered. These camps were sites of unimaginable cruelty, deprivation, torture, forced labor, violence, and disease.

Around 6 million Jewish men, women, and children were murdered by the Nazis and their **allies**. While the murder of Jewish people is what automatically comes to mind with the Holocaust, the Nazis also murdered millions of non-Jewish people, including Soviet prisoners of war, the Romani people, people with disabilities, Jehovah's Witnesses, German political opponents, LGBTQIA+ people, and Black people living in Germany and areas the Nazis conquered.

One of the main questions that arises today about the Holocaust is how was it allowed to happen? How were Adolf Hitler, his beliefs, and the Nazi Party allowed to rise to prominence in Germany?

There are several parts to this answer. First, Germany's democratic government was quite weak after losing World War I (1914–1918). It was unstable and unpopular among many Germans who blamed it for losing the war. In addition to this, the economic crisis of the Great Depression boosted support for **extremist** belief systems such those espoused by the Nazi Party, which led to Hitler's rise to power in 1933. Additionally, the Nazi Party harassed and imprisoned their political opponents in the concentration camps, creating fear among the German people, which silenced any form of **dissent**. This was further worsened by the fact that all political parties other than the Nazi Party were banned in Germany in 1933, preventing checks on Hitler's power and eliminating any institutions that could help stop him.

Before the Nazi party came to power in 1933, their **anti-Semitism** was no secret. As early as 1919, Hitler was writing about removing the Jewish people. In his book, *Mein Kampf*, published in 1925, he wrote of the Jews being an evil race, and the Nazi Party portrayed them as subhuman. This treatment of the Jewish people as not human

A destroyed business the day after Kristallnacht is shown here. This "Night of Broken Glass" was horrific, but the worst was yet to come.

would also come into play later in the concentration camps. (The Jews were portrayed as a race by the Nazis instead of a religious group. By portraying them this way, Nazi logic said they needed to completely destroy the Jewish race instead of focusing on converting them to another religion.)

When Hitler came to power in 1933, he started his destruction of the Jewish people by **boycotting** Jewish businesses. This was followed the next week by Jews being dismissed from civil service jobs, and within the same month, only a certain amount of Jewish children could go to school in German schools. The next month, Nazi students and professors removed tens of thousands of books from libraries and bookstores and burned them because they were "un-Germanic."

Discrimination against the Jewish people continued to increase in the years between the burning of the books and the burning of bodies in the crematoriums. By the late 1930s, Jewish people were desperately looking for countries to flee to, but most countries didn't want to accept such a large number of **refugees**.

On November 9, 1938, anti-Jewish violence erupted when more than 1,000 synagogues were ransacked, 7,500 Jewish businesses had their windows broken, and 30,000 Jewish men were arrested and sent to concentration camps. This night, known as Kristallnacht ("Night of Broken Glass"), was a turning point, laying the foundation for Hitler and Heinrich Himmler's "Final Solution," which was the Nazi's term for the deliberate **genocide** of the Jewish people.

CHAPTER ONE

LIFE UNDER NAZI RULE

With Adolf Hitler's rise to power in 1933 and the resulting discrimination against Jews, it was clear to many that they had no future in Germany. Their lives in Germany went from being normal citizens to extreme **marginalization** and increasing violence. In an interview, Margaret discussed how everything changed for her and her family in Germany, from being put in a ghetto to being moved to a concentration camp and then meeting the infamous Dr. Josef Mengele, who did many experiments on people in the camps.

FROM EXCLUSION TO DEPORTATION

Between 1933 and 1939, life significantly changed for the Jewish people in Germany. Their businesses were boycotted, they were stripped of their citizenship and defined as a separate race, and they were banned from professions such as trades, sales, and retail. Hateful **propaganda** portrayed them as inhuman, and eventually they had to wear a yellow Star of David on their clothing to identify themselves as Jewish.

Jewish people were eventually moved from their homes into ghettos in the late 1930s, and from there were transported to the camps. In her interview,

Scan this QR code to watch Margaret discuss her experience with Dr. Josef Mengele.

Hitler and a group of soldiers are shown here.

Margaret described the experience of being moved from her home to a ghetto to a camp:

> *[In] 1938, everything changed ... They decided to put us in a bigger city, [in a] ghetto. My whole family was there. But after that, we were divided. They put us on a special train, and that train took us to Auschwitz-Birkenau. It was an extermination camp.*

Jews were taken away in sealed cattle wagons on trains in very overcrowded conditions. There would often be more than 100 people crammed into single train car that was meant for 8 animals. People who were being deported didn't know what fate awaited them once they got off the train. The authorities disguised their true intentions by saying the purpose of the transport was to a labor camp or for resettling in the East.

The conditions in the cars were extreme. The journeys often lasted several days or even weeks, and people weren't provided with food or water. There was only one bucket for a toilet, which led to an awful stench. In the summer, victims experienced severe heat, while in the winter they experienced freezing cold temperatures. Many people died from thirst, exhaustion, or suffo-

Jewish people had to wear the Yellow Star of David, shown here, to show that they were Jewish.

cation before even reaching the camps. If anyone tried to escape, the guards were told to shoot them.

SELECTION PROCESS

Once the train arrived at the camp and the doors were opened, the Schutzstaffel (SS) officers would start shouting orders and hitting prisoners with their rifles. At camps like Auschwitz-Birkenau, prisoners immediately went through a selection process, which Margaret described in her interview:

Hateful anti-Jewish propaganda such as this poster were common during the Holocaust.

We had to be counted ... They took my mother and father out between me and my sister and they went on the left side. That's the last time I [saw] my parents. The people who were working in a crematorium told us what happened to the old people who went on the left side and their children: They were all gassed. Then they take them to the crematorium to burn their body. They

FAST FACT

HITLER BELIEVED IN A FICTIONAL "MASTER ARYAN RACE." THE TERM "ARYAN" WAS USED TO DEFINE GERMANS AND OTHER NORTHERN EUROPEAN PEOPLE. PEOPLE WHO WERE "ARYAN" WERE DESCRIBED AS HAVING BLOND HAIR AND BLUE EYES, EVEN THOUGH HITLER HIMSELF DIDN'T FIT THIS DESCRIPTION. THE "ARYAN" CONCEPT FREQUENTLY CHANGED AND WAS USED FOR PROPAGANDA AND SOCIAL CONTROL.

took us to the place to take a shower, and they shaved our hair and they gave us different clothes and shoes to wear.

The selection process often involved separating men and older boys from women and children. Then, the doctors, like Mengele, made brief inspections of each person and made quick judgements about their health and fitness to work. The main criteria for being able to work were age and physical fitness. Generally, if a child was under around

Jewish people being taken to Auschwitz would arrive at the gatehouse, which is shown here during a tour in 2023.

Once prisoners got off the crowded railway cars, they went through a selection process on the ramps. This would decide who was immediately sent to the gas chambers and who could work.

14 to 16 years of age, or if a person was elderly or sick, they were sent directly to the gas chambers. The victims were often lied to at this point and told they were going to the showers and for disinfection.

Those who were healthy and strong enough were sent to work. They were registered as prisoners, their personal belongings were taken, their heads were shaved, and they were forced to the real showers before being given a striped uniform and prisoner number.

FAST FACT

PRISONER NUMBERS WERE TATTOOED ON THE LEFT ARM AT ONLY ONE LOCATION: AUSCHWITZ-BIRKENAU. TATTOOS WERE ONLY GIVEN TO THOSE WHO WERE HEALTHY AND STRONG ENOUGH TO WORK. THESE NUMBERS REPLACED NAMES, LEADING TO FURTHER **DEHUMANIZATION**.

THE GAS CHAMBERS

There were about 50 distinct gas chambers in the camps. Other gas chambers were in the cargo areas of large vans. The gas chambers were the main way the Nazis carried out mass murder during the Holocaust. A gas chamber is a tightly enclosed room where people are killed by asphyxiation resulting from poisonous gas. Victims were tricked into going into the chambers because they were disguised as communal shower rooms. Those who couldn't walk from the selection area to the chambers were taken there in a truck. Everyone else marched.

When they arrived at the gas chamber, victims were told to take all their clothes off either in the yard or in a special undressing room if the chamber had one. Some camps had fake shower heads installed to complete the illusion that they were there to shower. After everyone undressed, they were led into the chamber and locked in, and pellets of Zyklon B (which was made up of hydrogen cyanide) were dropped into the room. Some camps used pure carbon monoxide in canisters or carbon monoxide from car engines instead. The gas killed victims within minutes, but sometimes took longer, and it was very painful.

After the victims died, other prisoners took their bodies out of the chambers and cut the women's hair, removed jewelry, and checked teeth for metal dental work, which was also removed. The bodies were then taken to pits or the crematorium furnaces to be burned.

Jewish people were deported to concentration camps on railway cars such as these.

The Nazis continued to murder people in the gas chambers through the very last days of World War II. They then tried to take down many of the gas chambers they created to try to hide the evidence of their crimes. However, not all the gas chambers were destroyed. For example, when **liberators** came to the Majdanek camp, they found that the gas chamber was nearly intact.

Empty canisters of Zyklon B pellets are shown here.

"ANGEL OF DEATH"

When Margaret and her family were going through the selection process, they encountered the infamous SS doctor, Josef Mengele, who was nicknamed the "angel of death." Margaret described her encounters with Mengele in her interview:

> *There was a doctor, his name was Mengele ... You [had] to go in front of him,*

FAST FACT

PRISONERS WERE FORCED TO WORK IN AND AROUND THE GAS CHAMBERS, REMOVING BODIES FROM THE CHAMBERS AFTER PEOPLE DIED, CLEANING THE CHAMBERS, TRANSPORTING PEOPLE TO THE CHAMBERS, AND TRANSPORTING DEAD BODIES TO THE BURNING PITS. THIS WORK DETAIL WAS KNOWN AS SONDERKOMMANDO.

undress, and if he sees anything unusual on your body, they put [you] to the side. He was doing twins experiments ...

I was there a couple weeks and I had on my body ... spots. It just came, and he was examining and thinking if he should put me in a place where he can study that. So luckily he just ... told me to go back in the line.

When he decided that he wants to do experiments, you [would] have to go with him, and he did whatever he wanted to do using all kinds of adult drugs. I know many people who were

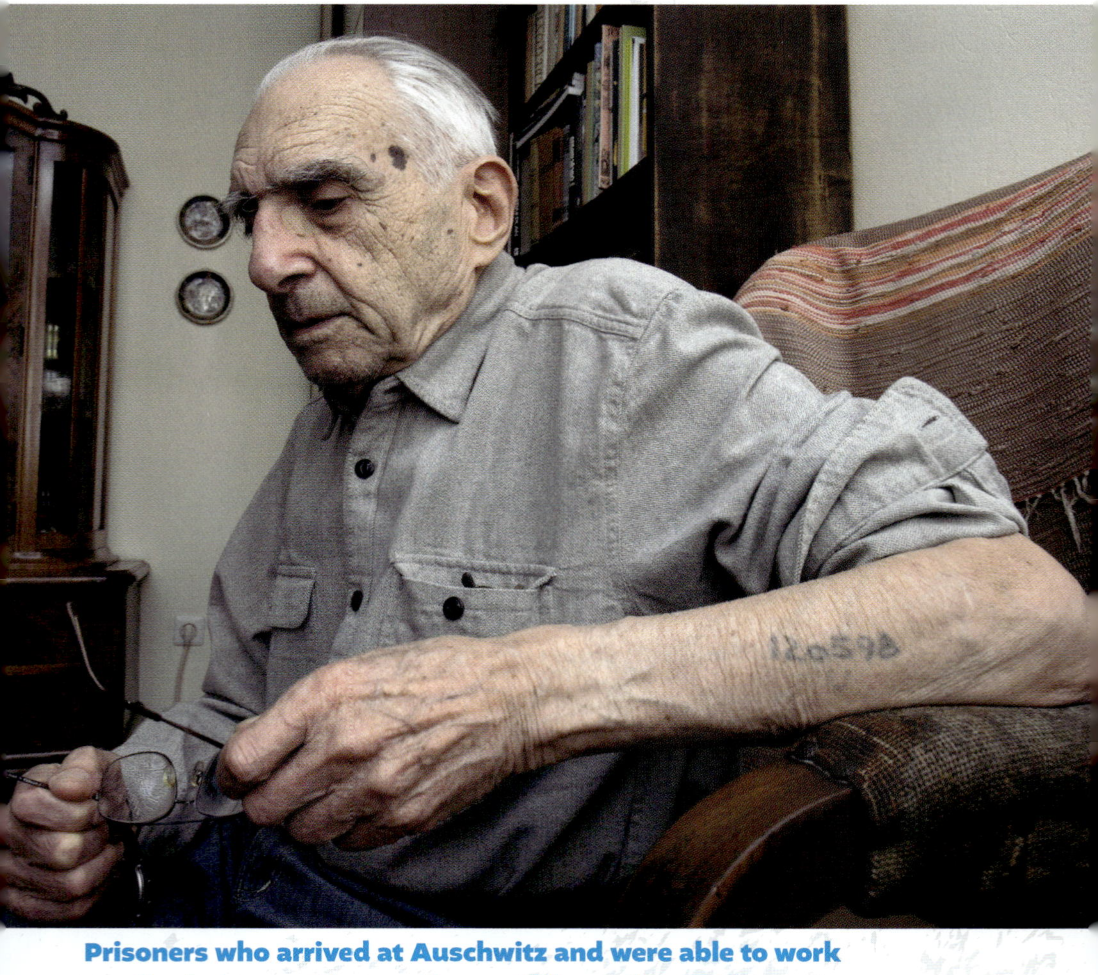

Prisoners who arrived at Auschwitz and were able to work received tattoos. The survivors still have them today.

The inside of a gas chamber at Auschwitz is shown here.

> *twins ... They liked to change them ... Mengele was the guy who always takes people ... to his office and examines them, trying to find out about the blue eyes with the brown eyes ... trying to do experiments.*

In popular media, Mengele is often portrayed as doing experiments without any scientific basis. However, the reality is worse: He was a medical researcher, a trained doctor, a war veteran, and respected in his field at the time. He worked in a leading research institute in Germany.

While studying in a university, he accepted the false idea of racial science and biological racism, believing "Aryan" Germans were biologically different from other races, and therefore superior to other races. In 1938, he joined the Nazi Party, and then in 1943, he was assigned to Auschwitz-Birkenau. Some evidence shows that Mengele requested to be sent there, however.

MENGELE'S EXPERIMENTS

Mengele was one of many doctors at Auschwitz-Birkenau and one of a dozen who performed experiments on the prisoners. The

Josef Mengele, shown here, is well known for performing unethical experiments on victims at Auschwitz.

experiments caused permanent harm or death, and sometimes causing people to die was the goal. The victims didn't **consent** to medical treatment, nor were victims told what would be done or the possible effects.

The experiments Mengele did included:

- infecting people with diseases to see what effects were caused and to test potential treatments
- performing unnecessary procedures or surgeries
- creating wounds on victims
- murdering and **dissecting**
- sterilizing victims (making it so they couldn't have children later in life)

Twins were an important part of Mengele's research, as Margaret noted in her interview. Mengele performed research on about 1,500 pairs of twins, and only about 200 pairs survived. He would perform research, often without anesthesia, such as removing blood from one twin and injecting it into the other, unnecessarily removing limbs or organs, and trying to change eye color to blue by injecting chemicals directly into the eye. This was very painful and often led to infections and blindness.

Mengele also did research on how genes impact physical and mental traits. This is an important area of research when done **ethically**; however, Mengele didn't ethically conduct his research, and the victims weren't aware of what he was doing. He was trying to see if there were chemical markers in the body that could identify the race of the person because he believed these markers were important for preserving the false idea of racial superiority of the "Aryan" Germans.

HOW YOU SEE HISTORY

1. How did Nazi laws and propaganda make it easier for people to accept the mistreatment of the Jewish people over time?
2. Mengele was a trained doctor but did unethical experiments. What does this tell us about how science and medicine can be misused when ethics are ignored?
3. Why do you think the Nazis used deception, such as calling the camps "labor camps" or disguising the gas chambers as showers?

CHAPTER TWO

ACTS OF RESISTANCE

As Nazi control expanded, Jewish families were forced into increasingly dangerous and uncertain situations. Ghettos were created to isolate and control the Jewish people, and many were later deported to camps where survival was unlikely. In an interview, Marian described being forced from her home into a ghetto, then being deported to three different camps, later escaping during the transport to the third camp.

TREBLINKA UPRISING

A key part of Hitler's "Final Solution" was moving the Jews from their homes to massively overcrowded ghettos. In the Warsaw Ghetto of Poland, approximately 400,000 Jewish people lived in 1.3 square miles (3.4 sq. km) of space, which resulted in about 7 to 9 people in a room on average. The conditions in the ghettos were poor, but they were just a holding place for the Jews until they were deported again.

Marian described the conditions of the ghetto her family was in:

September 1939 they chased us from our home. Beautiful home to a shack. We lived with rats. And then a few months later, they took away my father with my uncle. In 1942, they took all

Scan this QR code to watch Marian describe being taken from her home and eventually escaping the Nazis.

Very little remains of Treblinka today because Nazis tried to destroy evidence of their crimes. The site is now a memorial with a large central piece where the gas chambers were and thousands of stones with names of communities that victims were taken from.

the Jews to take us to Treblinka ... Thousands of Jews, young, old, men, and women.

Treblinka was one of the killing centers, or extermination camps, in the Holocaust. It started out as a forced-labor camp, and then the killing center was created in 1942. The labor camp became known as Treblinka I and the killing center as Treblinka II. The killing center was later taken down in the fall of 1943. In just over a year, personnel in the camp had murdered more than 925,000 people.

In 1943, Jewish prisoners there organized an uprising and resistance group. In August of that year, they took weapons from the armory, but they were discovered before they could take over Treblinka. Hundreds of prisoners tried to escape by storming the gate, but they were killed by the guards. More than 300 prisoners escaped, but many of them were tracked down by the SS.

In the fall of that year, Germans ordered that the killing center be taken down. Prisoners left in Treblinka were forced to take down

Watch towers enabled SS guards to watch the entire camp and prevent prisoners from escaping. A watch tower from Mauthausen that still stands today is shown here.

FAST FACT

THE GATE AT THE ENTRANCE OF AUSCHWITZ HAD THE PHRASE "ARBEIT MACHT FREI," WHICH MEANS "WORK WILL MAKE YOU FREE." PRISONERS IN AUSCHWITZ HAD TO WORK FOR MORE THAN 11 HOURS AT ONE TIME WITH LITTLE REST OR TOOLS. THEIR WORK INCLUDED MINING, SORTING BELONGINGS TAKEN FROM OTHER PRISONERS, MAKING WEAPONS AND CHEMICALS, AND LOADING HEAVY MATERIALS.

the camp and then were killed by guards after completing this task.

LIFE IN THE CAMPS

Marian's family was deported again shortly after arriving in Treblinka, missing the prisoner uprising. In her interview, Marian said:

A few months later they took us to Birkenau. To Auschwitz. Right away they gave us the numbers ... When we came to the first

Prisoners being taken to Auschwitz saw this gate, which can still be seen today.

camp ... this was a death camp where they learned to target shoot. And we were the target.

Daily life inside the camps was **brutal**. Prisoners were forced awake early in the morning and had to attend the *appel*, which was the daily lineup. They had to stand completely still, often for hours at a time, even in the wind, snow, and rain, and were subjected to violence from the SS guards. The appel took place first thing in the morning before forced labor, and then at night before

Prisoners had to stand for hours without moving during the appel.

Living conditions in the camps were horrible, and the barracks didn't offer protection from weather conditions. Barrack bunks at the Sachsenhausen camp are shown here.

the prisoners returned to their barracks after a small daily meal that often was made up of watery vegetable soup and a small piece of bread.

Majdanek was one of the worst camps when it came to living conditions. The wooden barracks didn't provide any protection from weather conditions, and before bunk beds were brought in, the prisoners slept on the floor or ground. The barracks didn't have a sewage system, and it was impossible for prisoners to wash their clothes or themselves—and prisoners

FAST FACT

THE TERM "CONCENTRATION CAMP" HAS BEEN USED UNIVERSALLY FOR ALL CAMPS, BUT THERE WERE CONCENTRATION CAMPS AND EXTERMINATION CAMPS. CONCENTRATION CAMPS WERE TO KEEP PRISONERS IN ONE PLACE WITH A DISREGARD FOR HEALTH AND INMATES' LIVES, WHILE THE PURPOSE OF EXTERMINATION CAMPS WAS JUST TO MURDER.

weren't allowed to have cleaning items, anyway. During the day, unshielded sewage pits were used as toilets, and during the night, large wooden containers were used as toilets inside of the barracks since prisoners weren't allowed to leave the barracks for any reason.

In Auschwitz, prisoners only had one uniform and uncomfortable clog shoes that caused sores. Prisoners had to wear this outfit day and night, even when it was lice-ridden. The barracks in Auschwitz also didn't protect prisoners from the cold, and their toilet was a single bucket in the barracks that was meant to serve hundreds of people. The Nazis claimed they provided a balanced diet for prisoners, but in reality the menu was close to what was offered in Majdanek: a bitter beverage in the morning (a coffee substitute), a thin soup of rotten vegetables or meat in the middle of the day, and a small piece of bread with margarine before bed.

Types of uniforms prisoners had to wear are shown here.

After prisoners were sent to the gas chambers, the crematoriums (shown here) were used to dispose of the bodies and hide evidence of the Nazis' crimes.

Even though conditions were terrible in the camps, prisoners found ways to resist and to document their lives. They'd write a diary on small pieces of paper, make drawings of camp life, conduct prayer services, and make jewelry out of copper wire.

VIOLENCE USED FOR CONTROL

Nazi authorities often used violence to control prisoners and prevent resistance. They used threats, beatings, and deadly force to create an atmosphere of fear and obedience. People were often executed publicly to send a message that anyone who disobeyed or tried to escape would be killed immediately.

Even though escape was extremely dangerous, some prisoners still resisted in any way that they could. Marian and her family were being deported from Auschwitz to the crematoriums at Mauthausen when she escaped from the train with her older sister Anna and three

CONDITIONS IN THE GHETTOS

Ghettos were a large part of dehumanizing, isolating, and then murdering the Jews. Many of the ghettos were enclosed by barbed-wire fences, walls, or both, like the Warsaw Ghetto, which was enclosed by a 10-foot-tall (3 m) fence that was topped with barbed wire. The purpose of the ghettos was to keep Jews separated from non-Jewish people and to have total control over them. It also made it easier to deport them to camps as part Hitler's "Final Solution."

The conditions in the ghettos were extreme and brutal. They were overcrowded and run-down, and the Jews could only bring a few personal items with them. Additionally, the German authorities provided minimal amounts of food, so thousands died every month from malnutrition. Children would often smuggle food through the walls surrounding the ghettos. This was the main way Jews in the ghettos were able to survive, but if anyone was caught doing this, it was punishable by death.

People were loaded on to cramped railway cars to be transported from the ghettos to the camps.

There was also no running water and little-to-no soap, and the sewage systems often didn't work. This led to garbage and human waste in the streets, which then led to contagious diseases like **dysentery**, **typhus**, and **tuberculosis**.

Jewish people were not allowed to leave the ghettos without special permits, and if they did try to leave without them, it was punishable by death. There were guards at the entrances to the ghetto and along the walls to enforce these rules.

A section of the Warsaw Ghetto wall is shown here. Parts of it are still standing today.

other women. They walked to a farm in Czechoslovakia. Marian said in her interview:

> *We never heard from Sonya [another woman in the camp] and my sister. We thought they all got killed ... A year later we heard from a person that my sister's alive and Sonya's alive.*

FAST FACT

PARTS OF THE WARSAW GHETTO WALL REMAIN STANDING TODAY. THE THREE PARTS OF IT THAT ARE BEST KNOWN ARE IN THE COURTYARDS OF HOUSING ON 55 SIENNA AND 62 ZŁOTA STREETS AND 11 WALICÓW STREET IN WARSAW, POLAND.

Survival after escaping often depended on help from others and hoping that they would choose to help instead of turning them in. Helping Jewish escapees was illegal and could result in severe punishment, including death.

This Danish boat rescued more than 7,000 Jewish people. Today, it's in the United States Holocaust Memorial Museum

Despite this, some people still provided food, shelter, and information, or helped escapees leave the country. For example, a rescue operation in Denmark helped more than 7,000 Jews by taking them to Sweden in small fishing boats.

HOW YOU SEE HISTORY

1. Marian said prisoners were used as "targets" in the camps. What does this tell you about how the Nazis viewed prisoners, and how does this connect to the idea of dehumanization?
2. Escape attempts often depended on the goodness of others. What risks did people face when they chose to help? What does this tell us about courage during the Holocaust?
3. Why do you think ghettos were used as a step before deportation to concentration and extermination camps?

CHAPTER THREE

A SYSTEM BUILT ON VIOLENCE

Concentration camps were places of forced labor, starvation, violence, and death right up until the last moment before liberation. Prisoners were stripped of their identities, choices, and possessions, and often forced to participate in and watch acts of violence. In an interview, Jack described arriving at Auschwitz as a prisoner, enduring starvation, being forced to participate in murder, and having his possessions and even teeth taken from him.

ELECTRIC FENCES AND DISEASE OUTBREAKS

Camps were surrounded by electrified fences, reminding prisoners that death could come at any moment. But it wasn't always the fences or gas chambers that caused death. As Jack said:

> *If you got within 8 feet to that fence, you got electrocuted ... You [could] get typhus. But you didn't have to get typhus to die.*

Extreme overcrowding, starvation, and lack of sanitation caused deadly diseases to spread quickly throughout the camps. Typhus, dysentery, and other illnesses killed thousands of prisoners. Medical care was almost

Scan this QR code to watch Jack discuss his time in Auschwitz and then later at the Nuremberg Trials.

The camps were surrounded by electrified fences and barbed wire.

FAST FACT

STARVATION WAS **INTENTIONAL**. FOOD RATIONS WERE MINIMAL ENOUGH TO KEEP PRISONERS WEAK BUT ALIVE ENOUGH TO WORK. HUNGER AFFECTED THE ABILITY TO THINK CLEARLY, RESIST ORDERS, OR HELP OTHERS, MAKING IT A POWERFUL TOOL OF CONTROL.

nonexistent, and sick prisoners were often ignored or killed. In addition, many died from malnutrition, starvation, or simply being worked to death.

FORCED PARTICIPATION IN VIOLENCE

The Nazis didn't just kill people directly. They also made prisoners take part in acts of violence against others. In his interview, Jack described the acts of violence he was forced to participate in:

> *I burned quite a few people alive ... They [used kerosene] to spray the people and give you a match ... [The guards would say,] "Throw the match, or we bury you."*

Prisoners were put into impossible situations, where refusing orders often meant death. By forcing prisoners to participate, the Nazis spread terror and **trauma** while also avoiding some of the responsibility themselves. Often, this group of prisoners, known as Sonderkommandos, were murdered after a few months of work because if the camps were ever liberated, the Sonderkommandos couldn't be alive to testify against the Nazis. The work they had

Camps were extremely overcrowded, with hundreds of people in one barrack. Overcrowded bunks at Buchenwald are shown here.

THE STORY OF ANNE FRANK

Anne Frank was a Jewish girl who, along with her parents, sister, and four other Jewish people, hid in a concealed annex in the back of a building. Anne was just 13 years old when they went into hiding, and they stayed there for two years until they were betrayed and the location of their hiding spot was given to the Germans. It's still unknown who betrayed the Franks.

Everyone in the annex was arrested and taken to concentration camps. Anne and her sister, Margot, were sent to Bergen-Belsen, where they died of typhus in early 1945, shortly before the camp was liberated. Their mother, Edith, died of starvation in Auschwitz. Their father, Otto, was also sent to Auschwitz and was the only surviving member of the family.

Just before going into hiding, Anne was gifted a diary for her birthday. She used this diary to write about the events in the annex and her feelings while growing up. The diary was found on the floor of the annex by Miep Gies (one of the people who helped hide the family) after Anne, her family, and the others hiding in the annex were arrested and taken to concentration camps. Miep Gies kept the diary in a drawer to give back to Anne after the war. However, when Anne's death was confirmed, Miep gave the diary to Otto Frank.

Otto published the diary as *Anne Frank: The Diary of a Young Girl* (more commonly known as *The Diary of Anne Frank*) in 1947, and it went

FAST FACT

WHEN SORTING THROUGH PRISONERS' LUGGAGE, THE BEST ITEMS WERE SENT TO GERMANY, AND LESS VALUABLE ITEMS WERE SENT TO *BEKLEIDUNGSKAMMER* (THE CLOTHING STOREHOUSE), THE *SCHUKAMMER* (WHICH STORED ALL THE TAKEN SHOES), OR TO *KANADA*, WHICH HAD GOODS FOR THE BLACK MARKET.

to do varied between camps, but often involved working in the gas chambers and participating in the killing process. They weren't allowed to warn incoming victims about the fate that awaited them.

THE THINGS THEY TOOK

One part of dehumanizing the prisoners was taking all their belongings. They were allowed to bring a limited on to become one of the most published books in the world. Before going into hiding, Anne made friends with another Jewish girl who was the same age, Eva Schloss. Eva's family also avoided imprisonment by hiding, but were also betrayed and sent to Auschwitz after two years in hiding. Eva and her mother survived the camp, but her father and brother did not. Eva later co-founded the Anne Frank Trust UK, a charitable trust made to help young people fight **prejudice**.

Years later, Eva's mother married Otto Frank. On January 5, 2026, Eva passed away, showing that we aren't that far removed from this horrifying time in history and that there are still people living who survived the Holocaust and remember these terrible times.

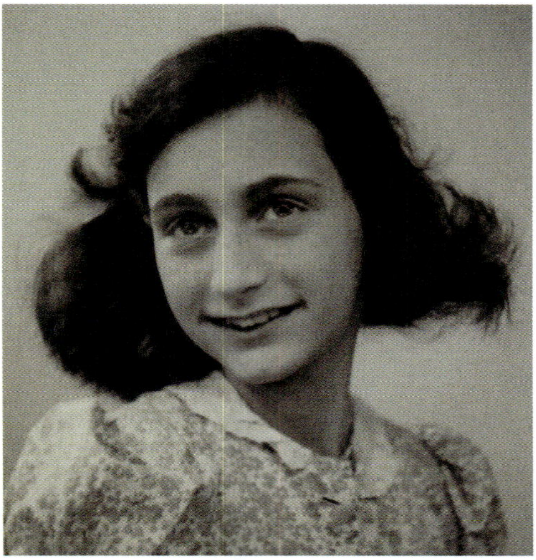

Anne Frank is shown here in 1942. It is the last known photograph of her.

number of travel bags, which people filled with clothing, bedding, footwear, personal documents, and valuables. Allowing prisoners to bring luggage kept up the illusion that they were working or resettling in the East. But once a train arrived at a camp, the luggage was taken and loaded on a truck to be sorted through later by Sonderkommandos.

Even the dental work prisoners had wasn't safe. In his interview, Jack described the lengths they went to in order to take the gold from his tooth:

> *I had a little gold filling on my tooth. Two guys from the line tied up my hands, gave another kid a pair of dirty, rusty pliers and pulled every one of my teeth from my gum to get that piece of gold from my crown down there. Since 17 and a half years old, I didn't have a tooth in my mouth. I didn't get infected, I*

Liberators of the camps found piles of shoes taken from victims, like the one shown here.

didn't die. My time was not up. [But] you couldn't get a sip of water to rinse your mouth.

"JUST FOLLOWING ORDERS"

As Allied forces advanced near the end of World War II in 1945, many camps were abandoned by the Nazis. Some prisoners were liberated, while others were forced on deadly marches or killed to hide evidence. For survivors like Jack, freedom came with lasting physical and emotional scars.

Everything was taken from victims in the camps. Thousands of wedding rings taken from victims are shown here.

After the war, Nazi leaders were put on trial for war crimes at the Nuremberg Trials, which aimed to hold individuals responsible for the crimes they committed during the Holocaust. However, some key people who were responsible were never brought to justice. Hitler took his own life in 1945 in a bunker when it was clear Germany wouldn't win the war. Mengele never showed guilt or acknowledged he was wrong, remaining a

FAST FACT

THE NAZIS USED **PSYCHOLOGICAL** TACTICS TO CONTROL PRISONERS. UNPREDICTABLE PUNISHMENTS, CONSTANT SHOUTING, AND SUDDEN CHANGES CREATED FEAR AND CONFUSION. PRISONERS NEVER KNEW WHAT WOULD HAPPEN NEXT, WHICH MADE ORGANIZED RESISTANCE DIFFICULT.

Victims entering the camps were allowed to bring luggage to keep up the illusion that they were just "resettling." But this luggage was taken and sorted through as soon as they arrived at the camps.

Nazi until his death in 1979. He escaped from being captured and brought to justice, living many of his final years in hiding. Heinrich Himmler bit down on a cyanide poison capsule after being captured by British troops to avoid going to trial for war crimes.

The Nuremberg Trials were held in this building, the Palace of Justice. It was chosen in part because it was where Nazi rallies were held, so it was seen as symbolic that the Nazi regime would come to an end in the same place.

The defendants' section at the Nuremberg Trials is shown here.

Jack was at the trials and questioned officers before they were executed. He said:

> *I don't care how high ranking an officer you were, you answered my question: How could you be out all day long, commit the* ***atrocities*** *that you have committed, then go home, touch your wife or touch your kid and even say "I love you." You know what the answer was? "On the orders of the Fuhrer."*

Many Nazi officials claimed they were "just following orders." The Nuremberg Trials rejected this defense.

Jack's experience shows an important lesson of the Holocaust: Obedience doesn't excuse cruelty, and moral responsibility can't be ignored.

HOW YOU SEE HISTORY

1. What responsibilities do people have when laws are unjust?
2. The Nazis took nearly everything from prisoners. Why was taking these items an important part of dehumanization?
3. Jack was forced to participate in violence under the threat of death. How does this help you understand the difficult choices prisoners were forced to make?

CHAPTER FOUR

DISCOVERY OF THE CAMPS

As Allied forces advanced into Nazi territory at the end of World War II, soldiers began discovering the full extent of the Holocaust. Reverend Wilson Canafax was among the first soldiers to enter Buchenwald, one of the largest camps. In an interview, he described what he saw when he entered the camp.

EVIDENCE OF MASS MURDER

Reverend Wilson first approached the camp on his own, unaware of what he would find. He had some free time and decided to approach a camp where he heard people had been imprisoned:

> *I guess we hadn't been fighting for maybe a week. I had a little time on my hands. I said I'd heard there was a camp down there close by where a lot of people were incarcerated. So I just went on my own and I was walking down the hill toward the encampment. A kid walked up to me and spoke excellent English, and he said, "I see you're a chaplain." He told me his name. He took me through the camp.*

The person Reverend Wilson came across was Elie Wiesel, a survivor who would later become a famous writer and a leading voice against genocide. Elie took him

Scan this QR code to watch Reverend Wilson discuss what he experienced upon entering Buchenwald at the end of World War II.

A train leaving Bergen-Belsen is shown here being liberated by Allied forces.

into Buchenwald, where he discovered evidence of the cruel control of the Nazis and the dehumanization of the prisoners. Many areas had already been partially destroyed as Nazis tried to cover their crimes, but enough evidence remained to see the scale of the atrocities. Many tools and spaces used for mass murder were still visible, as Reverend Wilson described:

> *There had been an old cleaning up. The killing walls were there. They had pegs on the walls up toward the ceiling, maybe 30 or 40 pegs around the room, and stools, and that's where they would put them and put nooses around their necks and kick the stools out from under them ... And when they all ceased to struggle, they'd cut them down and throw them in the ovens. When I got there, they quit the killing.*

Prisoner uniforms are one of the important artifacts of the Holocaust. Uniforms included a personal identification number and a badge that showed the prisoner's category.

FAST FACT

THE ALLIED FORCES WERE MADE UP OF SOLDIERS FROM A NUMBER OF NATIONS WHO FOUGHT AGAINST THE NAZIS AND OTHER AXIS POWERS, INCLUDING JAPAN AND ITALY. THE ALLIES INCLUDED THE UNITED KINGDOM, CHINA, THE SOVIET UNION, AND (AFTER 1941) THE UNITED STATES.

I stayed there for a while. I had arranged for worship services. The Jews, of course, had no places to worship. Their synagogues had all been destroyed or requisitioned or put out of existence. If you were a Jew, they just put you down in every way they could.

The "killing walls" Reverend Wilson described were used to hang prisoners as a way of murdering them.

PHYSICAL CONDITION OF SURVIVORS

As Reverend Wilson moved through Buchenwald, he saw prisoners who had survived the brutal conditions in the camp but were barely recognizable as human. Starvation, disease, abuse, and cruelty had left them extremely weak, and their bodies showed how much they had went through. In his interview, Reverend Wilson said:

FAST FACT

OBJECTS FOUND IN CAMPS, LIKE PRISONER UNIFORMS AND PERSONAL ITEMS, BECAME EVIDENCE IN WAR CRIMES TRIALS. THE **ARTIFACTS** HELPED PROVE THE SYSTEMATIC NATURE OF THE HOLOCAUST AND WERE DISPLAYED IN MUSEUMS TO EDUCATE FUTURE GENERATIONS.

Prisoners cheer for liberators at Dachau camp.

ELIE WIESEL

Elie Wiesel is a well-known author, activist, and Holocaust survivor. He's best known for his memoir, *Night*, which describes his experiences in Auschwitz and Buchenwald.

At 15 years old, Elie and his family were deported to Auschwitz then later deported to Buchenwald. His mother and younger sister died at Auschwitz in the gas chambers, while his father died in Buchenwald just before it was liberated. Elie and his two older sisters survived, leaving Buchenwald when it was liberated.

Elie later wrote about his traumatic experiences in the *Night* trilogy. *Night* was first published in 1956, only 11 years after the camps were liberated. The memoir was published during a time when not many survivors were talking about their experiences in the Holocaust, which made him one of the main witnesses of it. He dedicated his life to making sure people didn't forget the horrors of the Holocaust and spoke out against genocide and prejudice throughout his entire life.

Elie Wiesel, shown here, was among the first people to speak or write publicly about their experience as a prisoner in Buchenwald. He later became known as a leading voice against genocide around the world.

In 1986, he received the Nobel Peace Prize for his work against genocide and prejudice. He also helped establish the U.S. Holocaust Memorial Museum, which opened in 1993. Elie believed that he was spared from dying in the Holocaust and didn't want to **squander** the opportunity to make a difference in the world and ensure atrocities like that wouldn't happen again. Elie continued to fight against genocide and ensure the Holocaust wasn't forgotten up to his death in 2016.

They were all like zombies. They were ***emaciated*** *there. They look at their faces and they didn't know whether they were in a war time or what country they were in or whatever. They had been so neglected and underfed and persecuted and all that stuff that they didn't know whether they were living or dying.*

FAST FACT

LIBERATION DIDN'T INSTANTLY RESTORE NORMAL LIFE. SURVIVORS DEALT WITH LASTING PHYSICAL AND EMOTIONAL CHALLENGES FOR YEARS AND OFTEN FOR THE REST OF THEIR LIVES. THEY HAD TO COPE WITH MALNUTRITION, TRAUMA, GRIEF, SURVIVOR'S GUILT, AND DIFFICULTY TRUSTING OTHERS.

The survivors' physical conditions were difficult to observe. They had lost so much weight that their bones were visible under their skin. Being isolated, forced into **inhumane** conditions, and witnessing the atrocities and constant death created trauma that affected survivors' ability to understand the world around them. The suffering was both mental and physical, and these effects lasted long after liberation.

HOW YOU SEE HISTORY

1. Why might survivors' stories, like those of Elie Wiesel and the people interviewed in this book, be more impactful than statistics or official reports?
2. Do you think it's important for survivors to document their experiences of living through atrocities, even when doing so is painful and difficult? Why or why not?
3. How do physical artifacts from the Holocaust help people understand history more than just reading about it?

CHAPTER FIVE

BEARING WITNESS

Soldiers liberating the concentration and extermination camps weren't fully prepared for the horrors that they would find. Emaciated survivors and evidence of death defied belief. A former soldier who was among the first troops to reach Buchenwald described what it was like to see the aftermath of the Holocaust in an interview.

NAZI PROPAGANDA

The first moments entering Buchenwald were chaotic and shocking. In his interview, the unnamed man said:

> *Our division stumbled across Buchenwald, which was down near Weimar [in Germany]. And I say "stumbled across" because nearly all of them were stumbled upon by whoever supposedly rescued them ... The Weimar people claimed afterwards that they didn't know it was there; they didn't know what they were doing. But I find that hard to believe because they've burned people in the pits. And they're bound to have smelled something burning out there in the woods. So we never did believe that.*

Scan this QR code to watch a liberator of Buchenwald concentration camp discuss what they experienced when helping people in the camps after the Germans left.

After every barracks had been cleared at Bergen-Belsen, it was burned down to prevent the spread of disease.

Some local residents claimed they had no idea the camps existed or what was happening inside, even though evidence such as unusual activities or the smoke from burning bodies could be seen or smelled. The Nazis often used propaganda to disguise their true intentions and influence German and international audiences, saying that Germany was a victim of Jewish aggression. This claim supposedly justified war and violence against innocent people and portrayed an ideal future of national unity that was appealing to many Germans. The propaganda defended violence, saying it was necessary and morally defensible because

Germany was a victim and Jews and foreigners were a threat to this peace-loving nation.

Additionally, many details of the "Final Solution" were hidden from ordinary citizens, and restrictions on the press and media prevented citizens from reading about German crimes and Allied statements on those crimes.

Positive stories were also used to **deceive** the public. A booklet published in 1941 created an overwhelmingly positive picture of what the Nazi Party had done: It said Jews were put to work, clean hospitals were built, there were soup kitchens for Jews, and they received newspapers and career training. All of these claims were false. In addition, deportations from the ghettos were often referred to as "resettlements" to hide the fact that people were being taken to camps.

EMOTIONAL IMPACT ON LIBERATORS

Seeing survivors firsthand was deeply traumatizing to those who came to help. Prisoners were malnourished, ill, and traumatized, which made communication difficult. The horror that the liberators saw would stay with them for years. The soldier who helped liberate Buchenwald described the experience of walking into the camp:

> *The gate was open. The Germans were gone. They just abandoned these camps. When the troops came close to them, they just took off. There were dead people all over the place, and sick people laying on their bunks and whatnot, and racks of people, and some that were still running around. They were trying to catch the Germans who'd run off in the woods, trying to get rid of their uniforms.*
>
> *I went through the headquarters in there, and they had a room in there, a concrete room that had meat hooks hanging in the wall. And there were scratch marks on either side of the*

FAST FACT

THE FIRST MAJOR CAMPS WERE LIBERATED IN 1944 AND THIS CONTINUED THROUGH 1945. AS ALLIED FORCES ADVANCED TOWARD THE CAMPS, THE NAZIS EVACUATED PRISONERS TO OTHER CAMPS.

Liberators wore protective clothing when helping remove sick prisoners from the barracks of Bergen-Belsen to protect themselves from contagious diseases and lice.

> *meat hooks, which tells me that they hung the captured people by their chins on that meat hook. And they scratched those walls trying to get off of that thing. They were just unbelievably mean to people.*

The experience of liberating concentration and extermination camps left a deep impression on soldiers and aid workers. For many, the horror was difficult to process, and it created lasting emotional scars. Seeing survivors who were barely alive and the

ONGOING DISCRIMINATION OF THE JEWISH PEOPLE

One of the most difficult parts of learning about the Holocaust is discovering that to this day, Jewish people continue to face prejudice, discrimination, and violence in many parts of the world. Many countries were slow to provide assistance or recognize the unique struggles of survivors after the Holocaust, which made rebuilding their lives even harder.

Since the end of the Holocaust, anti-Semitism has persisted in different forms. Hate crimes, such as arson, attacks on people, and murder, and vandalism of Jewish cemeteries and synagogues continue throughout the world. Some people also falsely claim that the Holocaust didn't happen or minimize the impact of the Holocaust, which erases the experiences of millions of victims and survivors. After the war between Israel and Hamas began in 2023 and international groups began calling the situation a genocide of the Palestinian people, anti-Semitic incidents increased around the world.

Education and remembrance are some of the essential ways to fight against anti-Semitism. Organizations, museums, and memorials teach people about the Holocaust and the dangers of prejudice and hatred. By learning from history, people can recognize anti-Semitic language, **stereotyping**, and unfair treatment in the present day.

Remembering the Holocaust isn't just about honoring those who were lost and the experiences of those who survived and how they continue to have an impact. It's about ensuring that hatred and prejudice don't continue to harm anyone in the future.

FAST FACT

THE UNITED NATIONS DECLARED JANUARY 27 AS INTERNATIONAL HOLOCAUST REMEMBRANCE DAY. THIS IS THE ANNIVERSARY DAY OF THE LIBERATION OF AUSCHWITZ.

evidence of Nazi cruelty brought home the reality of the crimes against humanity that had been committed.

Many liberators didn't receive a warning of what they would see when they entered the camps, which made what they encountered even more traumatic.

Many soldiers have been unable to talk about what they saw when they liberated the camps because the trauma is too deep and there aren't words to describe the horrors they encountered, and they say it would be a disservice to those who survived.

Liberators who have chosen to speak about their experiences describe stacks of prisoners' bodies who were recently killed by Nazis;

FAST FACT

IN THE WEEKS BEFORE SOVIET FORCES ARRIVED TO LIBERATE AUSCHWITZ, SS PERSONNEL SENT MOST OF THE PRISONERS THERE ON A MARCH WESTWARD, WHICH BECAME KNOWN AS A "DEATH MARCH." PRISONERS MARCHED IN BRUTAL CONDITIONS AND WERE TREATED HARSHLY, AND MANY WERE MURDERED BY THE GUARDS.

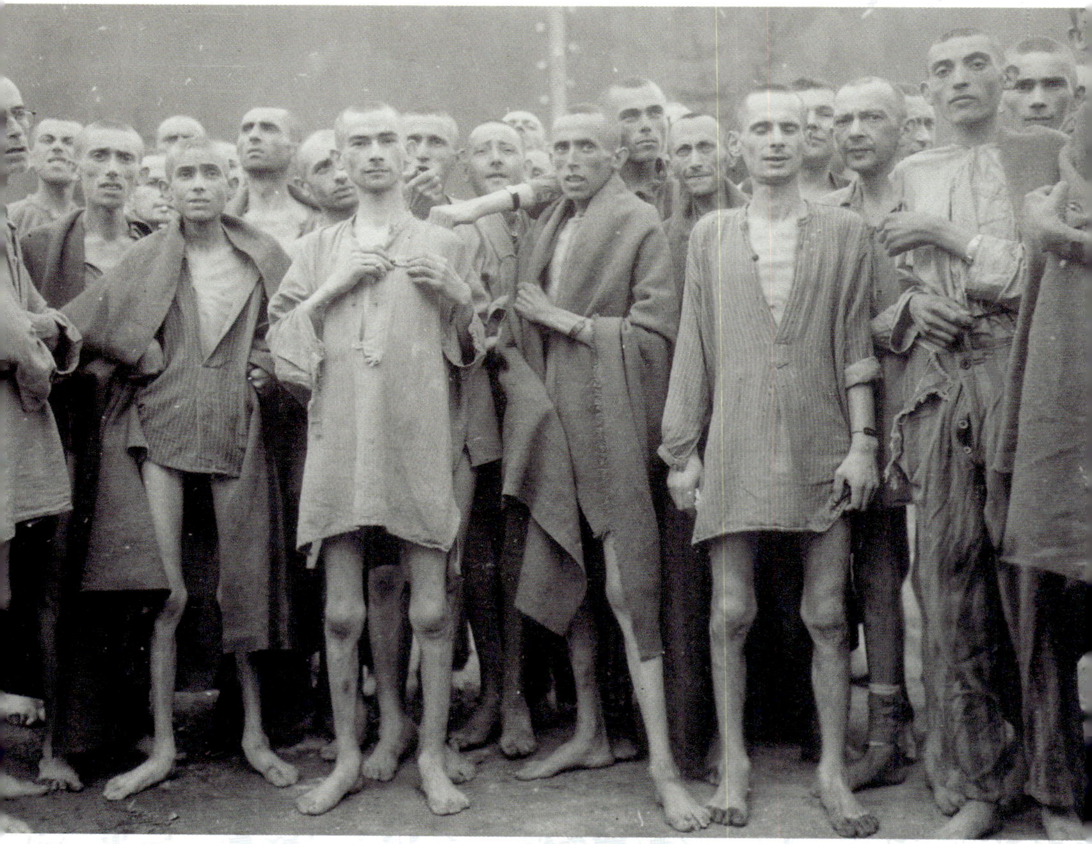

Prisoners, such as those shown here, were starved and emaciated, which took a very long time to heal from after liberation.

victims who were too weak to get up and go to the soldiers, so they hit a tin cup to get their attention; and victims who could only lay there so the only way to tell they were alive was their eyes.

THE LASTING IMPACT ON SURVIVORS

Liberation wasn't just a moment. It was a whole process. Many survivors faced ongoing mental and physical health issues, loneliness, and new challenges such as waiting in displaced persons' camps for years before they could immigrate to a new home. Many didn't return to their previous homes because of ongoing anti-Semitism and trauma from what they went through. The Nazis had taken away their careers, so they had to find new jobs. When they finally moved to a new country, they often had to learn a new language. And many didn't have any more family members to come home to because they had died in the camps.

Some survivors, like Elie Wiesel, shared their experiences through memoirs, diaries, and interviews to educate the world about what happened and to help ensure that the lessons of the Holocaust would be remembered and not repeated.

REMEMBERING THE HOLOCAUST: MEMORIALS AND MUSEUMS

Holocaust memorials and museums are incredibly important for preserving the memory of the victims, educating future generations about the atrocities that occurred, and working to ensure that nothing like the Holocaust ever happens again.

Former concentration and extermination camps like Auschwitz-Birkenau in Poland, Dachau in Germany, and Majdanek in Poland allow visitors to walk through the camp with guided tours. These memorials include preserved barracks, crematoriums, and gas chambers, providing evidence of the scale and horror of the Holocaust. Visitors can see personal items such as shoes, glasses, and suitcases from victims. The victims of the camps don't have graves. The only evidence of their lives are the possessions the Nazis took when they were forced into the camps and gas chambers.

A display of shoes that were taken from prisoners are shown here at a Holocaust memorial.

Upon arrival to the camps, the Nazis would shave the prisoners' hair off, which was later displayed in Holocaust memorial museums.

Museums like the United States Holocaust Memorial Museum in Washington, D.C., and Yad Vashem in Jerusalem, Israel, display artifacts with survivor testimonies, photographs, and historical documents. One of the most well-known exhibits in the U.S. Holocaust Memorial Museum is the collection of thousands of shoes from victims of the Holocaust. The Auschwitz-Birkenau Memorial and Buchenwald Memorial also have collections of human hair that was shaved and taken upon arrival to the camps.

Beyond preserving evidence of the Holocaust, memorials and museums are places for reflection and education. They encourage visitors to think about the consequences of prejudice, discrimination, and unchecked political power. Annual ceremonies, guided tours, and educational programs open the conversation about tolerance, human rights, and the responsibilities of individuals and governments.

By confronting the past directly, these memorials ensure the stories of survivors and victims aren't forgotten and remind the

Much of Auschwitz still remains today, allowing people to walk through it on tours and remember this horrifying time in history. An overhead view of the buildings is shown here.

Museums and memorials are essential for remembering victims and ensuring that atrocities like the Holocaust don't happen again. Visitors to the Unites States Holocaust Memorial Museum can walk through a cattle car, allowing them to experience a small part of the horror that victims experienced.

world that we must all actively work together to prevent atrocities like the Holocaust from happening now and in the future.

HOW YOU SEE HISTORY

1. How does ongoing discrimination of the Jewish people today show that the lessons of the Holocaust are still relevant?
2. Why do you think some Germans claimed they didn't know about the concentration camps, even when there was evidence of the camps and deaths?
3. How can people use what they learn about the Holocaust to stand up against prejudice and injustice in their own communities?

TIMELINE

LIFE UNDER NAZI RULE: TIMELINE OF THE HOLOCAUST

- 1933: Adolf Hitler rises to power in Germany.
- 1933: Restrictions on Jewish people rapidly increase.
- 1938: Doctor Josef Mengele joins the Nazi Party.
- 1943: Josef Mengele is assigned to Auschwitz-Birkenau and starts experimenting on prisoners there.

ACTS OF RESISTANCE: TIMELINE OF THE HOLOCAUST

- 1942: Treblinka II, the killing center, is built.
- 1943: A group of prisoners start an uprising in Treblinka.
- 1943: Treblinka II is taken down after the murder of nearly 1 million people in the killing center.

A SYSTEM BUILT ON VIOLENCE: TIMELINE OF THE HOLOCAUST

- 1945: Anne Frank and her sister, Margot, die of typhus in the Bergen-Belsen camp.
- 1945: World War II ends, and all camps are liberated.
- 1947: *Anne Frank: The Diary of a Young Girl* is published by Otto Frank.
- 2026: Eva Schloss, stepsister of Anne Frank and Auschwitz survivor, passes away.

DISCOVERY OF THE CAMPS: TIMELINE OF THE HOLOCAUST

- 1956: Elie Wiesel's memoir of the Holocaust, Night, is published.
- 1993: The United States Holocaust Memorial Museum opens.
- 2016: Elie Wiesel passes away.

BEARING WITNESS: TIMELINE OF THE HOLOCAUST

- 2023: War breaks out between Hamas and Israel.

GLOSSARY

allies: A group of people joined together in an activity or effort.
anti-Semitism: Hatred and discrimination toward Jewish people.
artifact: An item that remains from a certain time period.
atrocity: A shockingly horrific situation.
boycott: The act of joining with others in refusing to deal with someone or support a business as a form of protest.
brutal: Very bad, unpleasant, and severe.
consent: To give approval for something to happen.
deceive: To lie.
dehumanization: To treat someone like they are not human.
discrimination: The unfair treatment of a person or group because they are seen as different from other people or groups.
dissect: To take apart.
dissent: To not approve of or agree with something.
dysentery: A disease with severe diarrhea caused by an infection.
emaciated: Very thin and weak, especially from a lack of food or from illness.
extremist: Someone who supports measures or views that go beyond what is considered normal.
genocide: The systematic destruction of a group of people based on their race, culture, or views.
inhumane: Not how a human should act or be treated.
intentional: Done on purpose.
liberator: Someone who frees others.
marginalization: The movement of a group of people to an unimportant and powerless position.
persecute: To punish in a matter meant to cause harm.
prejudice: An unfair feeling of dislike toward a person or group because of their race or religious or political views.
psychological: Dealing with the mind.
refugee: Someone who flees from a country to escape danger.
squander: To lose something through inaction.
stereotype: To have an idea about a group that is untrue or only partly true.
trauma: Something that has caused severe emotional stress.
tuberculosis: A contagious disease that affects the lungs.
typhus: A contagious disease that involves headaches, fevers, and a rash. It's often spread through rats, lice, and ticks.

FOR MORE INFORMATION

BOOKS

Bitton-Jackson, Livia. *I Have Lived a Thousand Years: Growing Up in the Holocaust*. New York, NY: Simon & Schuster Books for Young Readers, 1997.

Frank, Anne. *The Diary of a Young Girl*. New York, NY: Bantam Books, 1993.

Mozes Kor, Eva, and Danica Davidson. *I Will Protect You: A True Story of Twins Who Survived Auschwitz*. New York, NY: Little, Brown Books for Young Readers, 2022.

Opdyke, Irene Gut, and Jennifer Armstrong. *In My Hands: Memories of a Holocaust Rescuer*. New York, NY: Ember, 2016.

Spiegelman, Art. *The Complete Maus*. New York, NY: Pantheon Books, 2011.

Wiesel, Elie. *Night*. New York, NY: Hill and Wang, 2006.

WEBSITES

Anne Frank House

www.annefrank.org/en/

The Anne Frank House museum website includes information on Anne Frank, the secret annex, the Holocaust, and topics related to the Holocaust such as democracy, prejudice, equal rights, and anti-Semitism.

Facts About the Holocaust

aboutholocaust.org/en

This website, a collaboration between the World Jewish Congress and UNESCO, includes photos and information on the ghettos, Nuremberg Laws, victims, and more.

Holocaust

www.britannica.com/event/Holocaust

This website includes thorough information on how Hitler came to power, the origins of the Holocaust, and the persecution of the Jews.

Holocaust Explained

www.theholocaustexplained.org/

This website, from the Wiener Holocaust Library, includes maps, timelines, survivors' stories, and more to present a complete introduction to the Holocaust.

United States Holocaust Memorial Museum

www.ushmm.org/

The official website of the U.S. Holocaust Memorial Museum includes information on the Holocaust, testimonies from survivors, videos, and more.

INDEX

PHOTO CREDITS

Cover, p. 29 Everett Collection/Shutterstock.com; p. 7 History and Art Collection/Alamy Photos; p. 9 Historic Image Archiver/ Alamy Photos; p. 10 D-VISIONS/Shutterstock.com; p. 11 German anti-Semitic and anti-Soviet poster/Wikimedia Commons; p. 12 Mo Wu/Shutterstock.com; pp. 13, 30 CBW/Alamy Photos; p. 14 Pe3k/ Shutterstock.com; p. 15 akturer/Shutterstock.com; p. 16 Imago/ Alamy Photosl p. 17 akturer/Shutterstock.com; p. 18 GL Archive/ Alamy Photos; p. 21 Maurizio Fabbroni/Shutterstock.com; p. 22 John Elk III/Alamy Photos; p. 23 Richard Bradley/Alamy Photos; p. 24 Pictorial Press Ltd/Alamy Photos; p. 25 Matyas Rehak/Alamy Photos; p. 26 UPI/Alamy Photos; p. 27 MPVHistory/Alamy Photos; p. 28 Archive PL/Alamy Photos; p. 32 Shawshots/Alamy Photos; p. 33 Buchenwald Slave Laborers Liberation/Wikimedia Commons; p. 35 Anne Frank passport photo, May 1942/Wikimedia Commons; p. 36 Everett Collection Historical/Alamy Photos; p. 37 Everett Collection Inc/Alamy Photos; p. 38 (top) Ruslan Kalnitsky/Alamy Photos; p. 38 (bottom) Marek Slusarczyk/Alamy Photos; pp. 39, 51 courtsey of the National Archives; p. 41 Holocaust train liberated by US Army/ Wikimedia Commons; p. 42 Stephen Barnes PL/Alamy Photos; p. 43 Prisoners liberation dachau/Wikimedia Commons; p. 44 Agence Opale/Alamy Photos; p. 47 The Liberation of Bergen-belsen Concentration Camp, May 1945 BU6599/Wikimedia Commons; p. 49 The Liberation of Bergen-belsen Concentration Camp, April 1945 BU4196/Wikimedia Commons; p. 53 (top) Andrew Sole/Alamy Photos; p. 53 (bottom) Holocaust-gas-hair/Wikimedia Commons; p. 54 Alexey Fedorenko/Shutterstock.com; p. 55 frederic REGLAIN/ Alamy Photos.

ABOUT THE AUTHOR

NICOLE HORNING is a published author of several nonfiction books for children and teens. She has her Bachelor's degree in English and a Master's degree in education. She doesn't just write for a living; she also enjoys it as a hobby. Nicole loves to collect books and read anything that sounds interesting to her. She also loves learning new things, especially historical topics. She does her best work while listening to Taylor Swift and having one of her two cats in her lap—both things happen a lot.